WRITTEN BY
JEFF LUCAS

JUL/AUG 2013

GW00691769

Are we nearly there yet?

Copyright © CWR 2013
Published 2013 by CWR, Waverley Abbey House, Waverley Lane, Farnham,
Surrey GU9 8EP, UK
Tel: 01252 784700 Email: mail@cwr.org.uk Registered Charity No. 294387
Registered Limited Company No. 1990308
Front cover image: Getty Images/Flickr/Photography by Paul Hollingworth
Concept development, editing, design and production by CWR.
Printed in England by Linney Print.

MIX
Paper from
responsible sources
www.fsc.org   FSC® C015900

HOW TO GET THE BEST OUT OF
LIFE EVERY DAY

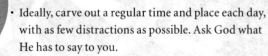

HERE ARE A FEW SUGGESTIONS:

- Ideally, carve out a regular time and place each day, with as few distractions as possible. Ask God what He has to say to you.

- Read the Bible passages suggested in the 'Big Picture' references. (As tempting as it is, try not to skip the Bible reading and get straight into the notes.)

- The 'Focus' reference then gives you one or two verses to look at in more detail. Consider what the reading is saying to you and what challenges that may bring.

- Each day's comments are part of an overall theme. Try to recall what you read the previous day so that you maintain a sense of continuity.

- Spend time thinking about how to apply what God has said to you. Ask Him to help you do this.

- Pray the prayer at the end as if it were your own. Perhaps add your own prayer in response to what you have read and been thinking about.

Join in the conversation on Facebook
www.facebook.com/jefflucasuk

AND so to Sinai. Having escaped the oppression of Egypt, and fought their first battle together, Israel gathers at the famous mountain. I imagine they had no idea of the huge implications of their gathering. What they thought was a temporary camp out in a mountainous area turned out to be one of human history's pivotal seasons. Here the foundations for Judaeo-Christian culture were established. Radical and compassionate values were hammered out here. If they were in any doubt that they were a people of destiny, Sinai should have resolved that once and for all. The Hebrews were not just evacuees, but pilgrims of purpose. And so are we: look at how many times Paul uses the word 'purpose' in Ephesians.

Sometimes I fear that we forget our purpose and identity. A signboard outside a church confirmed this: 'The next exciting event in God's schedule is the second coming.' When we think like that, life becomes dull and we wait for eternity to dawn. But that idea is wrong. The Sinai gathering was designed to show God's people how to live beacon lives that would startle, provoke and create enquiry from the rest of the world. Every day was meant to be spent living according to the Maker's design, unlearning the pagan ideas that had shaped their thinking and behaviour in Egypt, and marching to a different drumbeat.

Not every day is exciting for us. There are many boring bits to endure. But potentially the next purposeful event for God – and us, as we walk with Him by faith – is today, as we ask for grace to live life His way.

Prayer: Lord, be it exciting or mundane, help me to live for Your purposes today. Amen.

Saved for purpose

BIG PICTURE
Exodus 19:1–2
Ephesians 1:3–14

FOCUS
'On the first day of the third month after the Israelites left Egypt – on that very day – they came to the Desert of Sinai.'
(Exod. 19:1)

… how to live

beacon lives …

TUES 02 JUL

Law and story mingled

BIG PICTURE
Exodus 19:1–2
James 1:19–25

FOCUS
'On the first day of the third month after the Israelites left Egypt – on that very day – they came to the Desert of Sinai.'
(Exod. 19:1)

YEARS ago, our Sunday services called us to retreat from what was going on all around us, and the songs we sang reflected that. We were supposed to have a 'pure' spiritual experience on Sunday morning. Worship *does* give us the opportunity to pause, rest, reflect and put down our preoccupation with 'stuff' for a while. But the purpose of that pause is to recalibrate and refresh us for life in the real world. I've been in churches where breaking news of international disasters has been totally ignored, and no prayer or practical response has been offered, as if those cataclysmic events didn't matter. We had other more 'spiritual' concerns. But we're called to engage with world issues as we gather, praying for our leaders, and galvanising to serve our communities. Sunday mornings and Monday mornings should be as seamless as possible.

In Exodus, the Law was given as an integral part of the journey of God's people. They camped for 11 months at Mount Sinai, and as part of their trek, and in preparation for life in the coming promised land, they were given the wonderful gift of the Law. And the Law is woven into the narrative. This is quite unique in ancient Near-Eastern history.

God's revelation is for us as we travel forward in life. It is practical, relevant, and should never be treated as theory that we ponder at the weekend, but rather as truth to live in every day of our lives. And we prevent truth from becoming mere theory as, empowered by God's Spirit, we live obediently, applying today what we affirmed we believed last Sunday.

Prayer: Lord, empower me to live what I say I believe. I pray today for all in power around Your world. Amen.

MOST Christians come to the law-giving in Exodus having read the book of Romans first. Or perhaps we've been enthralled by Jesus in the Gospels as He fearlessly confronted the religious barons of His day, the Scribes and Pharisees. Famous for turning the Law into a confusing labyrinth of endless legislation, the Pharisees angered Jesus, who offered radical freedom from hollow, oppressive religion. But we can quickly rush to the idea that the Law itself was a burden, not a beautiful gift. Jews think otherwise, and to this day see the giving of the Law as an act of mercy. God's law is good, the psalmist insists. Far from leaving His people to their own devices (and we know where that leads), God provided clear structure for their lives, so that they could enjoy *shalom* – peace with Him, with others and with themselves. Abandonment is not a sign of love. Any parent knows that loves creates boundaries, not to inhibit but to protect.

Imagine if the government announced today that the laws of the land – all of them – had been suspended until further notice. Every citizen is now free to do whatever they like, no matter how evil. The judicial system is cancelled. None of us would venture outside, fearing the utter chaos that would ensue. Civil law is the basis of order and peace.

True freedom is not the absence of constraint, but a willing submission to standards and principles that have been outlined for our own ultimate good. Are we arguing with God, resentful of His demands and commands? Think again.

Prayer: Lord, help me to see that true freedom comes as I submit to Your loving rule in my life. Amen.

The Law as a beautiful gift

BIG PICTURE
Deuteronomy 6:1–25
Psalm 19:1–14

FOCUS
'The LORD commanded us to obey all these decrees and to fear the LORD our God, so that we might always prosper and be kept alive, as is the case today.' (Deut. 6:24)

God's law

is good ...

THURS 04 JUL

The Law: not just because I said so

BIG PICTURE
Exodus 22:21–27
Matthew 18:21–35

FOCUS
'Do not ill-treat or oppress a foreigner, for you were foreigners in Egypt.' (Exod. 22:21)

IT'S a classic example of poor parenting. The exasperated father barks an order at his child, who responds with the question beloved by small children: '*Why?*' The child isn't being rebellious, just inquisitive. The response is swift: 'Because I said so.' Parenting like that will oppress a child, stopping them from building a mature understanding of what is right and wrong. If anyone has the right to say 'Because I said so', it would be God. After all, He made us, we live in a universe of His design. He could demand absolute obedience for no other reason than that He has decreed it. Ours is not to question when He says jump, but rather just to ask how high the jump should be.

But that's *not* the way God deals with us, and it wasn't the way He gave His Law to the people of the Exodus. Israel's story gives birth to their Law. The Law makes sense because of their experience and, as we've seen, it is integrated with their story. And so, since they had been slaves back in Egypt, they are now commanded to be compassionate and just towards the disadvantaged. A similar idea is found in Jesus' story about the unmerciful servant, with the command to those who are forgiven to pass forgiveness around to others. Grace received should also be shared.

When we look back on our histories, we discover that God's way has been the right way. Not just because He requires our obedience, but because His infinite wisdom means that He sees what we don't see. His ways are the best way to go. If you are facing a decision – choose His way.

His ways are

the best ...

Prayer: Lord, thank You for the gifts of Your commands and constraints that are given for my good, and for the good of the community. Amen.

I'M SAD to say that it's happened to me too many times. Pressured by a bewildering array of sermons to prepare, deadlines to meet, people to see and bowed before a mountain of emails that await response, I live a chunk of my life living life *for* God but not really *with* God. Insisting that all these projects that keep me motoring away are surely His idea, I scurry on in my frantic existence. Perhaps it's an overstatement to describe it so bluntly, but it feels like a godless godliness. No morally suicidal decisions are taken, my ethics are generally intact. And I'm still serving, doing what I hope He wants. But there's little time for quiet, for whispered prayers or shared tears of frustration offered to Him.

In Exodus, God is the focal point both of the unfolding story, and the Law that is given. The Law is never presented as a cold, abstract morality code, but as an intrinsic part of the people's covenant relationship with their God. And God reveals Himself more and more, both in the people's experience as they travel with Him, and through the Law that He offers them. Not only are they called to do right but as they do, they understand more about the character of their righteous God. Worshipping God sits at the heart of the Law, and it all only makes sense when we realise that loving God with all our heart is the priority, as Jesus affirmed. Don't be so busy you miss the point. When we sing, 'It's all about You, Jesus', we declare a vital truth, and our lives will become shallow and empty if we don't live by it.

Prayer: Save me from Christ-less Christianity, Lord, from endless activity that was never Your idea. Help me to do the things You love. Amen.

The Law – God at the heart of it all

BIG PICTURE
Exodus 20:1–3
Matthew 22:34–40

FOCUS
'I am the LORD your God, who brought you out of Egypt, out of the land of slavery. You shall have no other gods before me.'
(Exod. 20:2–3)

The Law: responding to grace

We saw yesterday that the Law was never presented to the people as a 'law unto itself'. Obedience was a response to the mercy of God, not impersonal legislation. That's why I want us to ponder again those words about God bringing His people out of Egypt. Israel was called to live in a submission that was rooted in gratitude. It's an important distinction. When I obey the law of the land, I'm not doing so because I love the legislators who framed the rules in Parliament; I do what's required of me, because it's right.

But just as Israel was called to obey God in response to what He had done for them, so we are called to love because we have been loved first, to forgive because we have been forgiven, and not to be ashamed of Christ because He is not ashamed of us. God is the initiator of the covenant of law, and now of grace, and our grateful response is to follow and obey. That's why it's so important for us to remember what God has done, because as we remember, through prayers prayed and songs sung, so we respond with lives submitted to His love.

… remember what God has done …

To ponder: Is it possible that some of us don't respond to God with obedience, because we've not begun to grasp what He has done for us in Christ?

CWR MINISTRY EVENTS

Please pray for the team

DATE	EVENT	PLACE	PRESENTER(S)
5 Jul	Preaching Evangelistically	Waverley Abbey House	Andy Peck
5-7 Jul	Women's Summer Weekend	Pilgrim Hall	Lynn Penson
8-12 Jul	Seniors' Summer Holiday	PH	Derek & Margaret Martin
9 Jul	Help! I Want to Understand the Bible	WAH	Andy Peck and Lynette Brooks
9 Jul	Hearing the Voice of God	WAH	Andy Peck
13 Jul	Open Day/Commissioning Service	PH	
16 Jul	Mentoring Others	WAH	Peter Jackson
20 Jul	Insight into Forgiveness	WAH	Mary Higginson
8-12 Aug	Family Summer Holiday	PH	Jon & Sarah Stannard
10 Aug	Overcoming the Giants - Insight into Anxiety	WAH	Chris Ledger
12-16 Aug	Introduction to Biblical Care and Counselling	WAH	Angie Coombes and Team
27 Aug	Study Skills	WAH	Mary Higginson and Kathy Overton
28-31 Aug	Developing an Integrative Approach to Counselling	WAH	Mary Higginson
29 Aug	Handling the Pressure	WAH	Beverley Shepherd

Please also pray for students and tutors on our ongoing **BA in Counselling** programme at Waverley and Pilgrim Hall and our **Certificate and Diploma of Christian Counselling** and **MA in Integrative Psychotherapy** held at London School of Theology.

For further details and a full list of CWR's courses, phone +44 (0)1252 784719 or visit the CWR website at www.cwr.org.uk Pilgrim Hall: www.pilgrimhall.com

www.cwr.org.uk

The Law – God is an environmentalist

BIG PICTURE
Exodus 23:10–13
Psalm 24:1–2

FOCUS
'For six years you are to sow your fields and harvest the crops, but during the seventh year let the land lie unploughed and unused.'
(Exod. 23:10–11)

CONVERSATIONS about our Christian responsibility for the environment are commonplace these days – and that's good. Some sections of the Church have ignored the issue, partly because of an unhealthy view of the second coming of Christ. The idea is 'We're all leaving here anyway, and the planet's going to be burned up, so what's the point?' But the earth is not going to be trashed – just renewed. And it is selfish to say the earth doesn't matter – we are tenants here, not owners. And it ignores the plight of future generations.

Some Christians view *environmentalism* as a dirty word, because they have seen communities damaged by radical environmentalism that seems to care little about humans, but is weighted heavily to protecting species, ignoring totally the human cost. Living in Oregon years ago, I watched many people lose their jobs because a spotted owl was found in the nearby woods. Logging was halted for years. These issues are complex – but we should not overreact because we have witnessed environmentalism that ignored human concerns.

We can be guilty of limiting our thinking about God being the Creator to the events that happened in the beginning, when the earth was made, or perhaps to His provision of harvest, or offspring. But the Law given in Exodus is focused on the care and protection of the land, as well as those who live on the land. God's will is done in heaven, and through the Law, His rule was established on earth.

Biblical environmentalism is not just an idea whose time has come, but a timeless truth.

... we are

tenants here,

not owners ...

Prayer: Lord, help me to live as a steward of all Your gifts, and not as an owner. Amen.

LIFE involves a million choices. At the beginning of every day, as I make a bleary-eyed decision about the coffee cup I am going to use, I have to choose. As you read these words now, you have chosen to do so; you've selected a time, made a priority and decided not to do other things. Deuteronomy contains Moses' farewell speech to Israel, where he desperately sought to impress upon them the vital truths that they would need to remember in the promised land, for he would not be joining them for the journey. And so he calls the people to make choices between life and death. God's way brings life, and is the best way. It may be hard, but ultimately leads us to our true destiny.

When Adolf Hitler came to power, he gathered some leading pastors for a summit meeting. There he told them that their job was to get the German people to heaven – he and his regime would take care of everything else, effectively telling them to keep their noses out of politics and everyday life. Pastor Martin Niemoller spoke to Hitler afterwards, and boldly told him that the Church had also been given responsibility for the German people, and neither Hitler nor anyone else could take that away. That night, Niemoller's house was ransacked; the next day his home was bombed, then he was taken prisoner and held in custody for eight years. Niemoller chose well, even though it was a choice that led to pain and suffering.

Management consultant Peter Drucker says, 'Efficiency is doing the thing right, but effectiveness is doing the right thing.' How are our choices?

Prayer: Lord of life, Your way is the way to true life. Help me to choose well today. Amen.

The Law – calling the people to choose

BIG PICTURE
Deuteronomy 30:11–20
Deuteronomy 11:26–32

FOCUS
'Now choose life, so that you and your children may live and that you may love the LORD your God, listen to his voice, and hold fast to him.'
(Deut. 30:19–20)

The law and proof texting

BIG PICTURE
2 Timothy 2:14–15
Ephesians 6:10–17

FOCUS

'Do your best to present
yourself to God as one
approved, a worker
who does not need to
be ashamed and who
correctly handles the
word of truth.'
(2 Tim. 2:15)

AS WE begin to delve into the laws and principles that God gave to His Exodus people, we will find some alarming material. And we will learn that 'proof texting' – where Christians grab a verse out of the Bible, without any regard for its context – is dangerous. All of Scripture is given for us, but we must do the hard work of interpreting and understanding it. We must ask what it meant to those who first heard it, what the context and culture was, and realise that God was leading His people on a journey away from paganism into a new covenantal friendship with Him. We also need a wide-angle view of the whole of Scripture. It's said that a Bible text taken out of context is a pretext. If we don't understand that, we'll start selling our children into slavery (Exod. 21:7), executing Sabbath breakers (Exod. 35:2) and condemning footballers – touching the skin of a dead pig, from which footballs were traditionally made, makes one unclean (Lev. 11:8).

And of course, we need to understand the relationship between the old and new covenants, as Christ has wonderfully fulfilled the Law. Doing this hard work is not an attempt to water down the truth, as some try to suggest, insisting they just 'read the word and take it at face value'. That's like trying to read someone else's mail, without having any concern about who they were or what their circumstances were. Scripture today speaks to us, as we also understand how it first spoke. So put down that stone, and give that footballer a break. The Word of God is like a sword: mishandle it and people will get hurt.

The Word of God
is like a sword ...

Prayer: Help me to take the study of Your Word seriously, Lord, so that I might rightly apply it. Amen.

I'M EMBARRASSED to admit it, but in the earliest days of my Christian faith, I was usually at the church every time that the doors were opened – with the obvious exception of a ladies' meeting! There was, however, one event that I usually decided to give a miss – the missionary prayer meeting. A visiting missionary, armed to the teeth with 11,000 slides (or so it seemed) and a detailed biographical history of every one of the people in the blurry photographs, would treat us to what was quite honestly a dull presentation, after which we would spend an hour or so in boring prayer. It was not for me. But I regret my missional indifference. God is a missionary.

The exact location of Mount Sinai where the people of God gathered for 11 months is unknown, and the Jews seem indifferent about that. I find this refreshing, because too often 'holy' spots are turned into shrines, where the location itself is revered rather than the God who worked there. The whole thing then becomes just another must-see site in religious tourism. But commentators note that the giving of the Law in the wilderness points to the truth that God was not just blessing a specific nation with the gift of His Law, but was bringing this to the whole world. In that sense, the Law is not Israel's property. Let's remember today that God is not a Western God, or a Christian God, the God just for people like us, but He is the One and only true God of the whole earth. Mission matters, because God is a missionary.

Prayer: Lord, You love the whole world, impossible for me. Show me how I can play my part, and give me a heart that cares. Amen.

The missionary God

BIG PICTURE
Exodus 19:1–2
Matthew 28:16–20

FOCUS
'On the first day of the third month after the Israelites left Egypt – on that very day – they came to the Desert of Sinai.'
(Exod. 19:1)

The communicating God

BIG PICTURE
Exodus 19:1–5
Acts 17:16–34

FOCUS
'Now if you obey me fully and keep my covenant, then out of all nations you will be my treasured possession.' (Exod. 19:5)

ONE of the healthiest things that we can do, both as individual Christians and as churches, is to check our language. I'm not talking about swearing. I have sat through church services littered with 'the language of Zion' – phrases Christians are comfortable with, but which must create total bewilderment for those outside the Christian faith. When we ask people if they are 'washed in the blood' or 'redeemed', we can confuse rather than help.

Without sounding irreverent, the simple statement that Jesus saves could lead the uninitiated to think that He is a goalkeeper. We need language that will communicate. Churches must be aware that, as all communities quickly develop their own 'in' terms and vocabulary, they must be wary of this and seek to communicate in a relevant, contemporary and understandable way. What's all this got to do with Sinai? There God used a well-known sociological practice in the culture of the day – the establishment of covenant – to help His people to understand the relationship that He wanted with them. The Sinai covenant is set out as a suzerain treaty, a very familiar practice back then. So was the practice of circumcision, which was especially widespread in Egypt. Rather than rejecting a current cultural practice as being unholy, God the Holy One used that framework to communicate, and filled an existing human custom with fresh meaning and significance. We have not communicated unless we have been understood. Paul knew that when he used a pagan altar as a sermon illustration in Athens!

Prayer: Father, may my words not bewilder those outside the Church, while my life speaks with clarity of Your love. Amen.

13/14 JUL

Exodus 19:1–6 // 1 Corinthians 6:12–20

The God who treasures us

When we give our lives to Christ, we do just that – we hand over the rights and title deeds of our living to Him, in total surrender to His purposes. Our lives no longer belong to us – we are owned by Him. The massive implications of that choice are still being worked out every day, of course, as we offer ourselves to Him to fulfil all that *He* purposes through us. This choice affects the plans we make, the priorities we establish, and the way we treat our bodies. It is not our *days*, but the physical bodies we inhabit that are now His. All that we have is only lent to us – we are stewards of everything, entrusted with use by the owner. But while all the above is true, it's vital that we grasp that God does not 'own' us in the way that a rich person in bygone days might own a slave. Rather we are His 'treasured possession'. That speaks of tender care and loving affection. And let's always remember that, although it's true that God does own us individually, these words are written to the *people* of God. We find our destiny together, as part of the Church. We are cherished.

To ponder: What difference does it make to know that God not only owns us, but treasures us?

A kingdom of priests

FOCUS
'Although the whole earth is mine, you will be for me a kingdom of priests ...' (Exod. 19:5–6)

IT'S an idea that has surely been much misunderstood, and one that has hindered the Church through the ages. It's the misunderstanding of the priesthood. Let's be clear: leadership is God's idea, and He has given us leadership gifts in the Church. And there are countless faithful members of the clergy who are doing a sterling job as they sacrifice and sometimes endure in order to be faithful to their calling. But there's a danger that we forget that, in Christ, we are *all* called to be priests – if we forget that, then we will think that it is the task of the clergy to reach our world. They'll burn out while we get more critical! We are all called to priesthood. But what does that mean?

A priest brings the knowledge of God before the people. He or she is a servant rather than a ruler. They are bridge-builders between the world and God. But they are not just workers, but also worshippers. The word that is translated 'priest' here is not the expected word that describes one who officiates at a high place of worship, but rather one that has a right of entry to God. And now we have an even more illustrious calling, as 'royal' priests in the service of God.

Imagine it: if every Christian saw that they were called to walk with God, serve Him, and impact their world, then the work of mission would not be left to the overstressed few, but a vast army of ordinary people would impact the world with prayerful, loving acts of service. That's God's plan. And it always has been. Not just a few priests, but a kingdom of priests.

Prayer: Lord, bless and strengthen those who lead, and empower and envision us to play our part in the kingdom of priests that You have created. Amen.

HOLY. It's a much-maligned word. I remember as a new Christian being tagged as a 'holy Joe' at school. I didn't really understand what holiness was, and besides, my name is Jeff, not Joe ...

Holiness is not like a fragile flower, but a potent force. When Jesus came into contact with great evil, rather than running from it, He ran towards it, and demons screamed in the face of His awesome holiness. And holiness is not a negative thing. Sometimes I hear Christians use the word *holiness* and then go on to list the things that they no longer do, as if holiness is just about prohibition. Of course, holiness will cause us to say 'no' to things that we know are wrong – but the holy person or nation is not just called to be separated *from* certain habits and ideas, but also separated *to* the purposes of God. We are set apart for His agenda and will.

Holy: we need to redeem the word. To live a holy life is to experience what it means to be healthily human. It's the best and most fulfilling way to go. A truly holy person is not an otherworldly, weird and socially awkward soul, but a rounded, whole person who is attractive in their lifestyle. Jesus is the ultimate example of holy humanity – and sinners loved to be around Him. That alone should challenge our confused thinking about what holiness is and make us ask the obvious question – how popular are we with the 'wrong' crowd? Or do we bear a more striking resemblance to the pseudo-holiness popularised by the Pharisees? They didn't have too many party invitations.

Prayer: Mighty God, shape me into being a truly healthy, holy human being – and save me from false piety and legalism. Amen.

A holy nation

BIG PICTURE
**Exodus 19:1–6
1 Peter 1:13–16**

FOCUS
'... and a holy nation.'
(Exod. 19:6)

We are set

apart ...

Whatever

BIG PICTURE
Exodus 19:8
John 2:1–12

FOCUS
'The people all responded together, "We will do everything the LORD has said." So Moses brought their answer back to the LORD.' (Exod. 19:8)

IT'S a word that children sometimes use these days when they're being discourteous or dismissive to their parents: *whatever*. In a single word, the frustrated parent is being told that whatever they have to say, whatever authority they may try to exert, it's all white noise to the child: it's all irrelevant. Whatever.

In the vocabulary of the children of God, the word has an entirely different meaning. Notice that as the Israelites pledge obedience to what the Lord demands, they do so before they hear the full details of His plans and strategies for them. Obedience is not about deciding that what God asks is palatable and doable; rather we surrender to the as yet unknown will of God before it is revealed to us. Prior surrender is the key. Or, to borrow the language of Mary to the stewards at the wedding at Cana, 'do whatever He tells you'.

This last week I met Tom Paterson, who is a man who exemplifies this attitude of surrender to the *whatever* of God. Losing his 12-year-old daughter Debbie to spinal cancer, Tom made a decision then to surrender to the goodness of God, whatever God might ask of him and whatever might come his way. Tom has since lost two other children and his wife. Now a frail 87-year-old, he exudes the quiet strength of one who has gone way beyond a faith that is full of words and ideas, but has ruggedly trusted God through the valley of the shadow of death. We don't know what's ahead today, never mind tomorrow or next year. But God give us grace to say with Israel, and with Tom: whatever.

... do whatever

He tells you

Prayer: Lord, my prayer is simply this: whatever. Amen.

ONCE again, we see God the communicator in these verses. He didn't need all of the cloud and smoke and fire to accompany His presence, and when you look carefully at the book of Genesis, He appears without the epic backdrop. The picture of God strolling in the Garden of Eden is beautiful in its simplicity, and this approach continues through Genesis. It's only in Genesis 15:17 that a dramatic, arresting phenomenon takes place. But this was what the people would have expected. If a human king revealed himself with much fanfare, how much more would a divine King? God went to great lengths to communicate to people with methods, images and words they could easily understand.

That speaks volumes about the heart of a God who is desperate for people to know Him. God is passionate about reaching everyone on this planet with the news of His love and the offer of life through Jesus Christ. He is not passive, waiting, available but unmoved. Rather He is the God who runs out, using every method at His disposal to turn our heads and our hearts. The parable of the prodigal not only portrays a God who comes running, but who uses a number of props to communicate His love for His returning son, as He brings him a ring, robe, shoes – and lunch. Sometimes it's easier to believe that God is passionate and filled with love for the world, than to accept the wonderful truth that this is how He feels about *me*. Perhaps you experience the same struggle. May something of that wonder grip your heart and mind afresh today.

Prayer: I'm grateful, Lord, that You use so many methods to get our attention. May the reality of Your love fill our hearts and minds. Amen.

Royal protocol

BIG PICTURE
Exodus 19:9–13
Luke 15:11–32

FOCUS
'The LORD said to Moses, "I am going to come to you in a dense cloud, so that the people will hear me speaking with you."'
(Exod. 19:9)

God is not anti-sex

BIG PICTURE
Exodus 19:9–15
1 Corinthians 7:3–5

FOCUS
'Then he said to the people, "Prepare yourselves for the third day. Abstain from sexual relations."' (Exod. 19:15)

ALONG with talking about money, teaching about sex is likely to get a Christian leader into trouble. Christian writers can get into hot water if they determine to talk honestly about it. Recently I wrote a hard-hitting piece about the Hollywood glamorisation of sex. But one reader quickly and publicly wrinkled his nose, as if open conversation about sex is always inappropriate.

As God tells His people to refrain from sexual relations as they prepared to encounter Him on the mountain, we could rush to a similar view: sex is not quite holy, sex is tainted, and therefore indulging in it is met with an air of disapproval from God. But how untrue that is. The people were called to abstain from celebrating their human relationships because they were to focus on a history-altering encounter with God. The Lord was not disapproving of the sexual act, which, after all, is His ingenious invention. A similar approach is called for in 1 Samuel 21: holiness requires that we are set apart for God's purpose, and so in a season of encounter or warfare, a temporary period of sexual fasting might be called for. The New Testament supports this idea, but gives strong warning about extremism. Certainly the principle of enforced celibacy for priests is not found here, although of course anyone may embrace singleness and celibacy if they feel this is their specific calling. God does not disapprove of sex, but as the inventor of it, calls us to express and enjoy it in its right context, marriage.

Prayer: God, grant me purity, without unhealthy piety; help me to celebrate what You give, but never misuse Your gifts. Amen.

Endorsement

Before we leave this chapter let's notice that God was seeking to offer clear endorsement to Moses, especially in verse 9.

Leadership often evokes mistrust these days. During last year's presidential election campaign in America, truth checkers stood by during the televised debates, to question or validate the statements made. In the UK, politicians no longer enjoy the same level of trust as before the expenses scandals of a few years ago. That's a tragedy, as many of them are passionate people who entered public service to help make the world a better place. Mistrust of leadership has obviously touched the Church too, from abuse by priests to the harrowing tales of bullying by some leaders.

All this said, a leader can only function in their calling when they are given a mandate to do so. They can only lead if people will follow. God wanted the people to trust Moses, and so this dramatic encounter was staged, in part, to enable God to 'endorse' His candidate for leadership. The Father did the same for Jesus at the Mount of Transfiguration. Pray for those who lead.

God wanted the people to trust Moses ...

To ponder: How can we trust our leaders but at the same time ensure that we don't help create a culture where they can abuse their authority?

vital:

Bible teacher Phin Hall is passionate about helping people know and understand the Scriptures. In a new series of books called *Vital*, Phin explores spiritual disciplines and how they can encourage a deeper love for the God we serve. We caught up with Phin to find out more …

[CWR:] What drew you to write the *Vital* series?
[Phin Hall:] The roots of this series go back to my days as a youth worker, when the young people jokingly insisted my answer to everything was, 'Read the Bible and pray'. Behind the joke, however, was a genuine desire to understand why these disciplines were so important and if there were other things they could do to help themselves as young Christians. So I set about investigating what was so vital about these practices and what else might assist our walk with God.

What was your vision for the series as you began to write?
In life in general, my primary desire is to walk well with God and help others to do so too, so really this has been my vision for the series. The books are for anyone who wants to grow in their love for God and in their life as one of His children, and I have tried to write them in such a way that they would be beneficial both for group and individual study, together with discipling partnerships.

Which disciplines do you cover and how did you select these?
The areas of spiritual discipline I have chosen for this series can be grouped into three areas. Firstly, our focus on God, through worship, fellowship, simplicity, solitude and silence;

Phin Hall

secondly, our focus on Bible study, giving, submission and thanksgiving; thirdly, our focus on ourselves; and finally, our focus on daily life and living for today.

It may all sound a bit contrived and convenient, but these areas of spiritual discipline have been practised for thousands of years by godly men and women, and have been proved of great worth because they bring us into closer relationship with God – and that is ultimately what Christianity is all about.

Also available in eBook/ Kindle formats

Vital: Worship
Worship, Fellowship, Simplicity, Solitude/Silence

Vital: Bible Study
Bible Study, Giving, Submission, Giving Thanks

by Phin Hall
£4.99
Available April 2013

Scan with your smartphone for video introduction to material on *Vital*.

or visit www.cwr.org.uk/vital

Free video teaching from Phin available to download for each session

The Ten Commandments

BIG PICTURE
Exodus 20:1–17
1 John 4:7–21

FOCUS
'And God spoke all these words: "I am the LORD your God, who brought you out of Egypt, out of the land of slavery."'(Exod. 20:1–2)

AS WE begin to look at these most famous words, we'll consider a couple of important foundations. First, let's not succumb to the notion that because we are not under law, the Ten Commandments are of no relevance. On the contrary, through the operation of grace and by the work of the Holy Spirit, we are to live these commandments out at the deepest level. Secondly, let's reject the myth that the people of Israel were saved *through* these commandments. This revelation was given to a people who had already been rescued. They did not earn their deliverance by the keeping of rules. Instead, they were called to abide by these standards in response to the deliverance freely given to them. So it is with us: we are saved entirely by grace, and so our obedience to the purposes of God comes out of gratitude, not servitude. And then let's realise that the commandments are about both living *for God*, and living *with people* – the two are intertwined. So when we look at the New Testament, we see that we are called to love God, and demonstrate that love for God who is invisible by our love for the irritating person that we occasionally wish was invisible …

This last point is vital, because some Christians insist that they are deeply committed to Jesus but display an arrogant attitude. I wonder just how close to Jesus they really are. Love for the Lord should produce love for people: it's true in the Ten Commandments, and it's true in the teaching and ministry of Jesus. May it be true in our own lives today.

Prayer: Lord, enable me to hear the heart behind the Law, and change my heart to reflect Yours. Enable me to love You, and to love others. Amen.

THE Ten Commandments are often seen on plaques in the home of Christians – but often with the first two verses left out. Yet they are absolutely vital, setting the context for everything that follows. The Ten Commandments are not impersonal rules arbitrarily imposed upon people, but are given in the context of God's relationship to His people – He is their God, and therefore calls them to echo His character in their behaviour. And He is the God who has brought them from slavery to a new freedom, and now invites them to ensure that they live obediently and respectfully so that everyone can experience peace. As we hear that He is the God 'who brought you out of Egypt, out of the land of slavery', we hear a very commonly used phrase in the Old Testament – it is used no fewer than 124 times. In ancient culture, no other 'god' made such a claim: they were now called to be a loyal people, in response to God's loyalty and faithfulness to them.

Having assured the people that they belonged to Him, now God lets them know that as God, He belongs to them. He is their God, not in a territorial way that implies that they have the exclusive franchise on God, or that they can control or manipulate Him, but that He is utterly committed to them, and freely entwines Himself in their history and future. In Christ we see the fulfilment of this truth, as Christ loved us and gave Himself for us. Let's offer ourselves as willing sacrifices today: God has laid everything on the line for us.

Prayer: Thank You, Lord, for showing me what true love is: You loved us and gave Yourself for us, and to us. Amen.

Much more than laws

BIG PICTURE
Exodus 20:1–2
Romans 12:1–2

FOCUS
'And God spoke all these words: "I am the LORD your God, who brought you out of Egypt, out of the land of slavery."' (Exod. 20:1–2)

… offer ourselves

as willing

sacrifices …

He comes first

BIG PICTURE
Exodus 20:3
Matthew 6:25–34

FOCUS
'You shall have no other gods before me.'
(Exod. 20:3)

THE first commandment establishes the foundation that must be in place: Israel was commanded to make God their absolute priority, and offer unwavering love and loyalty to Him. Remember that they lived in a culture where a whole smorgasbord of gods was available. Here, God does not set out to either prove or disprove the existence of other 'divine' entities – that is done elsewhere in Scripture as lifeless idols are exposed for what they are. And the word that is used here could also describe supernatural beings that are not gods, like angels and demons. Rather, God instead simply lays down the foundation for all life: Him first. And just as Israel battled with the temptation to take their worship elsewhere, so will we. One translator suggests that a good rendering of this verse is 'You shall not prefer other gods to me'. Sometimes other priorities come to us with very definite appeal; they are alluring, and we are slowly drawn away.

This commandment is echoed in the New Testament as Jesus sets out His kingdom charter, and calls us to 'seek first the kingdom of God' – a metaphor for the rule and reign of God. Unless that decision has been made in our lives, and then remade every day, then Christianity won't make sense. Following Jesus is the right way to live, but is a terrible hobby. God doesn't want to be an addendum or an extension for us, a helpful religious compartment to help us to get through our tougher seasons. Rather, He is to be our purpose, our priority, our commander, our friend, our Lord.

Following Jesus

is the right way

to live ...

Prayer: Surrender requires strategy, Lord, not just a moment of emotion. Help me to place You as Lord of my life today. Amen.

EARLIER I mentioned that in giving Himself to us, God does not invite us to manipulate Him. But to try is a common human failing. One of our greatest temptations is to try to make God into what we want Him to be, rather than accepting Him for who He is. As we hear God prohibiting portraying Him as an image, we need to understand the cultural context for these words. In those days, it was believed that if a person possessed an image of a god, then he had power to control that god. In his wonderful book *The Trivialization of God: The Dangerous Illusion of a Manageable Deity*,* Donald McCullough points out that we so easily drift into this sin – imagining God to be what we want Him to be. He talks about a lady called Sheila who developed what she called 'Sheilaism'. 'I believe in God. I'm not a religious fanatic. I can't remember the last time I went to church. My faith has carried me a long way. It's Sheilaism. Just my own little voice.'

McCullough goes on to list some of the 'gods' that we can try to make God into: the god of my cause (I'm passionate about this, hence so is He), the God of my experience (this is what happened in my Christian life, so it must be real), the God of my comfort and my success (who only exists to make me happy), and the God of my nation (I like where I live, so God must think that my nation is the centre of the earth too). Let God be God.

Manipulating God

BIG PICTURE
Exodus 20:4–6
Isaiah 46:1–13

FOCUS
'You shall not make for yourself an image in the form of anything in heaven above or on the earth beneath or in the waters below.'
(Exod. 20:4)

Prayer: Shatter the false idols in my thinking. Grant me a greater understanding of who You really are. Amen.

*Donald McCullough, *The Trivialization of God: The Dangerous Illusion of a Manageable Deity* (Colorado Springs: NavPress, 1995) p.67.

The name

BIG PICTURE
Exodus 20:7
Exodus 9:13–16

FOCUS

'You shall not misuse the name of the LORD your God, for the LORD will not hold anyone guiltless who misuses his name.'
(Exod. 20:7)

FOR a few moments, I didn't want to be a Christian. I was watching a television interview with a spokesperson for a 'church' in the USA that continually expresses hatred for gay people, and insists that God hates America. Every time a soldier is killed overseas, they celebrate what they see as the judgment of God. They are infamous for picketing the funerals for fallen soldiers, brandishing their 'God hates you' signs. As I listened to the smiling spokesperson, I realised that it was not just the actions of her group – it was the terrible damage that she was doing to the name of God that alarmed me. The third commandment is not just about blasphemy, although it includes it. There is always a danger that we use God's name as a mantra. Others use God's name to underscore the truth of what they are saying, whereas the Christian is called to a consistent honesty so that no one would have any reason to doubt the integrity of their words. But this commandment is primarily about reputation; how we make God look by the way we live.

A real challenge to those of us who profess to know Him, and insist that we do what we do in His name, is that people look at us, our attitudes, our words, our tone and assume that God is like us – an awesome and frankly terrifying responsibility! A major reason for the Exodus and the creation of the 'people of God' was that God's name be known in all the earth. Let's live today in a way that uplifts and honours the name of the God whom we love and serve.

Prayer: Help me to speak, to act, to serve, to respond, in a way that brings glory and honour to Your name, Lord. Amen.

27/28 JUL

Exodus 20:8–11 // Colossians 2:16–23

Sabbath

It's called a Sabbath lift, and I discovered it while in a hotel in Israel. Because strict Jews believe that completing an electrical circuit on the Sabbath involves work, the lift is programmed to automatically stop at every floor so that no buttons have to be pushed. While I don't doubt the sincerity behind this, it does make God seem to be very picky indeed. Is this really what God intended with His call to remember the Sabbath day by keeping it holy? Certainly the principle of Sabbath – the pause for rest, replenishment and worship – has been built into creation, and we ignore it at our peril. But let's also know that in Christ our 'Sabbath day rest' has been established, and He is the Lord of the Sabbath. The Sabbath was always intended as a gift, not a burden, and now the keeping of individual days is a matter of personal conscience (Rom. 14:15) because the OT Sabbath has been abolished (Gal. 3:24–25; Col 2:16). God is a God of rhythm. When we ignore that, we shouldn't be surprised if our bodies – and our society – suffer as a result.

To ponder: Do you treat the concept of Sabbath as a vital principle or a luxurious option?

... He is the Lord of the Sabbath

MON 29 JUL

Honour your parents

BIG PICTURE
Exodus 20:12
Ephesians 6:2

FOCUS
'Honour your father and
your mother, so that you
may live long in the land
the LORD your God is
giving you.'
(Exod. 20:12)

I HAVE mentioned before in *Life Every Day* that my
family is currently battling against dementia, which
continues its wicked onslaught on my mother. As
I write these words, I am preparing to fly back to
the UK to visit her; she is now in need of full-time
professional care. It has been one of the greatest
challenges of my life, to know how to respond
respectfully and graciously when the disease takes
over and conversation becomes very fraught indeed.
But as I read these words, I'm challenged once again
about what is important to God. Generally thought of
as an exhortation to adults rather than small children,
and therefore specifically relevant to those of us with
elderly parents, the command contains a revolutionary
truth that would have been shocking in Moses'
culture: it was the mother as well as the father who
should be honoured.

The word *honour* is not so much about obedience
but speaks more of concern, respect, thoughtfulness,
affection and appreciation. And then there is the rest of
the statement, which effectively says that the quality and
even longevity of life will be improved for those who obey
it. This is not a magic formula for a long life – be nice to
your parents and you'll be an octogenarian – as many
who have done their best to fulfil this commandment
have not magically escaped premature death. But we see
that when honour is woven into the fabric of our family
relationships, so life will be less stressful, more fulfilling,
and therefore often longer in time and greater in quality.

**Prayer: Lord, help me to be honourable, when it's
tough. May I bless and encourage seniors whom I
meet. Amen.**

IT'S a hotly debated issue, especially in the light of the ongoing debate around capital punishment. Living in America, just last night I received news of another execution by lethal injection in Texas, with two more scheduled in the coming weeks. Opponents of capital punishment often appeal to this verse to support their opposition to the judicial death penalty. While we may argue against the death penalty for many reasons, including the possibility of error and the lack of evidence that it truly is a deterrent, we cannot use these words for support. Likewise, arguments for pacifism or against abortion should be stated without appeal to this verse. Unfortunately the AV and the RSV translations of the Bible rendered this as 'You shall not kill' but the word used here is never used in the context of human warfare. Israel was commanded to use the death penalty in a limited way for certain crimes. The verb here is always used in the Old Testament of 'illegal' killing. What is prohibited here is murder, and the rationale behind the command is that life is the gift of God, and is not ours to take away.

Jesus expanded these words in the Sermon on the Mount, teaching us that the way that we speak of others can 'kill' them, damaging their reputation and their quality of life. It's possible to murder a person's hope and sense of self-worth, without resorting to violence. While this commandment makes a very specific statement about actual murder, it's possible to commit a crime but still leave someone with a pulse.

Prayer: May I be a bringer of life and love, Lord. Save me from the sin of character assassination. And when I am angry, may I not sin. Amen.

Murder

BIG PICTURE
Exodus 20:13
Matthew 5:21–22

FOCUS
'You shall not murder.'
(Exod. 20:13)

… life is the gift of God …

Adultery

BIG PICTURE
Exodus 20:14
Matthew 5:27–30

FOCUS
'You shall not commit adultery.' (Exod. 20:14)

IN A world that uses the term 'casual sex', we must know that God's attitude to sex is anything but casual. Adultery is committed by married people or, at least, by one married partner. Again Jesus would later expand the teaching of this commandment to condemn mental adultery. With the accessibility of pornography, these words are strikingly pertinent. As we reflected earlier, God is not anti-sex, nor does He prohibit it. In giving the beautiful gift of sex, He sees its potential for great joy and celebration – and great devastation. Adultery erodes two basic building blocks of society – marriage and family.

While absolutely upholding this standard, let's also reflect on Jesus' attitude towards the woman caught 'in the very act' of adultery (John 8). He didn't demand that the other party be brought out for punishment; He neither excused the adultery nor suggested divorce, but offered forgiveness and grace.

A word about 'emotional affairs': I know that it's possible to clearly cross a line and become connected with someone in a way that is wholly inappropriate. I have heard people say that an emotional affair is just as bad as an actual affair. This might lead people to think, if what they have already done is as bad as a physical affair, why not just go ahead and indulge their passions anyway? And that's deception. If you've crossed a line into an emotional attachment, but not an actual physical affair, there's a way back. Take it while you still can.

Prayer: Lord, protect the relationships I enjoy from even a hint of immorality. Help me to be a person of clarity, grace, and compassion. Amen.

No thieving

BIG PICTURE
Exodus 20:15
Ephesians 4:25–28

FOCUS
'You shall not steal.'
(Exod. 20:15)

IT'S a terrible feeling that anyone who has suffered a burglary understands. It's not just that what belongs to you has been taken by someone else, and so you feel aggrieved by injustice: you have worked hard to get those items, and now someone else has just plundered your property. There's something deeper – a sense of personal violation. A stranger has been in your home, invaded your private space – and your life feels bruised and fragile as a result. The ancient Hebrews understood that idea, and viewed a person's 'stuff' as an extension of their self. A crime against property was a crime against the owner.

Because the Bible views work as a gift from God, and not just a means to an end, theft is a usurping of that God-given means to gain, and violates the dignity of the person who has been stolen from, as well as the thief himself. Notice that when Paul writes to the Ephesians, he not only calls the thief to stop stealing, but to start working *and* giving.

And there are more ways to steal than just by breaking and entering. When we in the West charge developing nations exorbitant interest rates, are we stealing from them? What about the maverick traders who, without permission, foolishly gamble with their clients' money on high-risk strategies, or banks that lend their investors' money to unqualified mortgage applicants, knowing that they were more likely to default?

And here's a subtle 'stealing' practice sometimes found among 'good' Christians – borrowing something, and not returning it.

Prayer: Grant me the privilege of honest work in order to provide, Lord; and of honesty in my dealings, and integrity in all my ways. Amen.

… the Bible views

work as a gift

from God …

Speak the truth

FOCUS
'You shall not give false testimony against your neighbour.' (Exod. 20:16)

THERE'S no such thing as a little white lie. As God commanded integrity of speech, it was initially in the context of judicial proceedings. When lies are told in court, the full force of the justice system comes crashing down on the one falsely accused. Punishment in Old Testament times could be swift and merciless. But the command had wider applications: we've already seen that a person's good reputation can so easily be stolen. This often happens in churches, where sexual immorality is rightly frowned upon, but those who gossip (or 'share widely' as some would call it) go unchallenged. Once a person's reputation has been violated, it can take a lot of work to correct the injustice, and when people insist that there's no smoke without fire, it never is fully remedied. Jesus again extended the idea to say that we should be people of truth at all times. I don't take His words to mean that I can't take an oath in court – Jesus responded to one at His trial, and God frequently bound His covenant with an oath in Scripture. But as a Christian, my word should be trustworthy.

And then, when it comes to gossip, let's remember the rather obvious fact that the gossip needs an ear in order to spread their slander. According to an old rabbinic saying, slander 'kills three: the one who speaks it, the one who listens to it, and the one about whom it is spoken'. To borrow a line from Shakespeare, when the gossip says, 'lend me your ear', we should refuse, lest we become guilty simply by listening.

Prayer: Lord, in my speaking, and in my listening, help me to be a person of the whole truth. Amen.

I want what you've got

There are some who look at the Ten Commandments and then Jesus' expansion of them in the Sermon on the Mount, and then conclude that the old covenant was just about outward behaviour, while the new covenant is about heart attitude and change. But the command against covetousness shows us that God was always concerned with addressing what we felt and thought on the inside, as well as our outward behaviour. While we may congratulate ourselves that what we actually do before other people might look good, God calls us to go deeper – to consider our inward desires, what we want. Covetousness cannot be tested for or policed: it happens in secret. God alone knows what is going on. Do we truly celebrate with others who are blessed with what we'd love to have, but don't possess?

Ambition is not coveting; it is not wanting to get on or even have more that is condemned (although it's all too easy to slip from ambition to wanton greed) but rather it's wanting more at the expense of others, or even taking what they have: that is coveting.

To ponder: In talking about sin to the Roman Christians (Rom. 7), Paul especially points to covetousness. Why do you think he did that?

… God calls us
to go deeper …

JEFF AND KAY ON TOUR

This November Kay and I are off to the Holy Land, and we'd like to invite you to come along with us!

As well as taking in some of the wonderful, inspiring sights of Jerusalem, and enjoying the simple beauty of Galilee, we'll be tracing some of the footsteps of Samson, the dubious 'hero' of my recent book, *There are No Strong People*.

I'll be sharing from the Samson story each day, and we'll be visiting some key biblical locations, amongst them several particularly associated with Samson.

Touring starts in the Beit Shemesh area visiting the sites at Tel Tzora and Eshta'ol. Eshta'ol is thought by many to be the grave of Samson. We'll also go to Ashkelon, where Samson mounted an attack, and see ruins that actually predate the headstrong muscle man, including the oldest arched gate in the world, which was built by the Canaanites.

Heading further south we'll visit the Hebron Region and Tomb of the Patriarchs – one of the least disputed spots in Israel and a truly special site – and Tel Romedia, closely associated with both Samson and Delilah.

There will be time to stop for photos on the summit of the Mount of Olives and the chance to sing in St Anne's (with the pool of Bethesda in its garden) an unbelievable experience – as well as a visit to the Israel Museum with its many artefacts dating from the Samson period. Yoel Nesson, until recently the Academic Director of the

IN THE HOLY LAND

International School at the Hebrew University, and an internationally recognised biblical archaeologist, will give a talk about the new scientific evidence supporting the biblical account, and lead a Q & A session.

Together with an excursion to Galilee visiting well-known places such as Nazareth and Capernaum, and a boat trip on the Sea of Galilee, the last full day will offer relaxation at a Dead Sea Spa with mud baths (rumour has it they will make you ten years younger – now I'm ready for that!) and hot sulphur baths (will clear up skin infections and many other conditions due to natural antibiotics). And of course there will be the opportunity to swim in the Dead Sea. This concluding day will also include a visit to the site where David spared Saul's life.

The dates for the tour are 3–10 November 2013. Come along! For details call Chris on 01938 561604 or email chris@travelinkuk.com

Kay and I would be delighted to have you with us.

MON 05 AUG

FOCUS

'Moses said to the people, "Do not be afraid. God has come to test you, so that the fear of God will be with you to keep you from sinning."'
(Exod. 20:20)

… He is God

… and we

submit to Him

AT FIRST glance, it seems like Moses is contradicting himself – on the one hand, he tells the people not to be afraid – and then he calls them to fear God.

We are all pendulums, swinging wildly from one extreme to another, usually in response to hurt. People are totally committed to a church, give their lives to seeing it built. Then someone upsets them, and they leave, maybe withdrawing from meeting with others at all. Some of us walked in the charismatic tradition, and genuinely met God, but then some extreme madness crept in, and so we swung away and now act as if the gifts of the Holy Spirit are not for today at all.

In the same way, we can oscillate between a terrified fear of the awesome power and might of God and an inappropriate familiarity with Him. We *can* come to Him with confidence – the writer to the Hebrews makes that clear. Recently, I heard of a Christian who was offended at a worship song that proclaimed 'I am a friend of God'. Jesus makes it very clear – He does not call us servants but friends (John 15:15). But the opposite extreme of this is a casual attitude where we forget that we are talking about God, not a friend whose sole purpose in life is to make us feel comfortable. As has often been emphasised, the 'fear' of God is a reverential attitude towards Him. Reverence doesn't mean a pious voice, a hushed silence or a religious posture, but true reverence acknowledges that He is God, we are not, and we submit to Him. God was not looking for a cowering people, but a loving, respectful people.

Prayer: Help me to draw near to You, Lord, and know the friendship that is mine through Christ. Banish any terror, as I revere You. Amen.

IT WAS one of those rare, gloriously hot English summers, and I was attending my very first Christian youth camp. As the temperatures climbed, so the amount of clothing worn around the campsite lessened. Soon there were complaints, and a few of the young men on the site complained to the leaders that they found the girls playing volleyball in their bikinis 'distracting'. When this was mentioned, the ladies rightly retorted that the short shorts that the lads were wearing (this was the seventies) were distracting to them too! A measure of common sense – and common decency – was needed by both sexes to ensure that the camp ran smoothly. It sounds a little odd to say it, but here goes: I am so glad that we live in days where people don't feel the need to 'dress up' for church gatherings. But at the risk of sounding like someone who takes too much notice of these things, sometimes I've seen worship being led by men and women who were offering a little too much distraction by the way they were dressed.

As we consider the foundations of the Law given to the Israelites, it's clear that God thought that these things mattered. While we aren't called to dress up, we are commanded to dress in a way that isn't provocative. And for those who say that the problem is with the one who does the looking (and that's partly true), we're reminded that we shouldn't give undue cause for a stare. While not being legalistic or prissy about these things, let's be thoughtful about these issues and use our common sense.

Prayer: Lord, protect my mind, my eyes, my thoughts. And in these and in all matters, help me to use some common sense. Amen.

Common sense

BIG PICTURE
Exodus 20:22–26
1 Timothy 2:8–10

FOCUS
'And do not go up to my altar on steps, or your private parts may be exposed.' (Exod. 20:26)

WED 07 AUG

People are not things

BIG PICTURE
Exodus 21:1–11
Galatians 3:26–29

FOCUS
'If you buy a Hebrew servant, he is to serve you for six years. But in the seventh year, he shall go free, without paying anything.' (Exod. 21:2)

I KNOW. I don't like it either. All of this talk of slavery is utterly jarring. Why didn't God just outlaw the practice of slavery? William Wilberforce, in trying to combat slavery, had to face Bible-believing Christians who waved these texts, together with Paul's instructions in the New Testament about slavery, and insisted that slavery was biblical. All of this forces us to face the need for us to read the Bible with some understanding of the cultural context in which it was written. Slavery was such a common practice in Moses' day that the entire system rested upon it. And in New Testament times, with countless slaves contributing to the mighty Roman Empire, a call to abolish slavery would have been tantamount to a call to revolution, inviting even greater persecution than the Church was already experiencing. It seems that God was gradually weaning people away from the concept of slavery, and in the book of Exodus gives unparalleled rights to slaves, who, in the wider culture of the day, were considered to be things, totally without rights, rather than human beings whose needs had to be considered.

Let's not just be frustrated by the slow pace that God had to take to gradually wean His people away from slavery – let's ensure that we help those who are trapped in human trafficking, which is going on now all around us. As we look back with frustration at the injustices of the past, let's not ignore the very real plight of millions of modern slaves in the present.

Prayer: Lord, may I never treat people as objects, rather than people to notice. And bless those who campaign today to set captives free. Amen.

WHEN you read this list of penalties, it is harsh: the world the Hebrews lived in was a rough place. But as we look at this list of crimes and punishments, we realise that God was absolutely committed to having His people stand head and shoulders above the rest of the world, not in arrogant pride, but with an amazingly high level of integrity that would have turned heads and hearts. As we saw when we considered that God wants the goodness of His name to be proclaimed by those bearing His name, that means we are called to live to a higher standard. And for those who would embrace the privilege and calling of leadership, the standard is yet higher.

It's tragic when Christians abandon principles of love, grace, integrity, punctuality and respect, and just settle down into living without a care in the world. To be brutally honest, the cost of discipleship can get tiring, which is why Paul challenges the Galatians not to 'become weary in doing good' (Gal. 6:9). There are times when I frankly don't want to be bothered with doing the right thing. But when that happens, there's more than personal erosion and damage in my life. I end up being like everyone else, and unrecognisable as a child of God. The salt has lost its savour, and the light on the hill is hidden. In the pressure to be accessible and relevant, let's never lose sight of the truth that we are called to be different, not because of superficial legalism, but because of hearts that genuinely want to be holy.

Prayer: When doing what is right seems tiresome and too costly, remind me of who You have called me to be, mighty God. Amen.

To whom much is given

BIG PICTURE
Exodus 21:12–36
Romans 12:1–2

FOCUS
'If anyone uncovers a pit or digs one and fails to cover it and an ox or a donkey falls into it, the one who opened the pit must pay the owner for the loss' (Exod. 21:33)

… we are called

to be different …

FRI 09 AUG

BIG PICTURE
Exodus 22:1–15
Philippians 4:1–3

FOCUS
'Whoever steals an ox or a sheep and slaughters it or sells it must pay back five head of cattle for the ox and four sheep for the sheep.' (Exod. 22:1)

THE laws that God gave to His people were not just concerned with punishing right and wrong, but also sought to bring restitution to those who had been wronged. Not only did God want to prevent exploitative behaviour, but to bring peace and restoration to the relationships that were shattered by crime. It's apparent from this that when damage was done by the sins of a person, that was not to be the end of the matter: healing and reconciliation was to be sought. In a small community context, people were likely to encounter each other frequently; these laws called people to do more than apologise, but to rebuild broken relationships with action.

We're called to take a similar attitude when our relationships break down. Conflict is inevitable in the close-knit communities of our churches; gather any group of human beings together in close proximity, add the fuel of our passionate opinions and convictions, and then consider the diversity of the church (many of us wouldn't be together for any other reason except our common experience of the love of God) and there are bound to be disagreements. But sadly, sometimes conflict is the signal for some Christians just to walk away and join another church. Repairing relationships is costly, time consuming and humbling – but it's better than just tossing years of fellowship and friendship aside, as if relationships and church affiliations are disposable items that have little value for us.

When – not if – we fall out with each other, let's seek repair rather than rushing to retreat.

Prayer: Lord, help me to work hard to restore relationships, when I am hurt, or when I have hurt others. Amen.

Exodus 22:16–19 // Exodus 7:8–13

Run from the occult

In verses that, again, are difficult, notice that God deals with sorcery and bestiality together. In a culture where it's fashionable to treat spirituality as a buffet, and we pick and choose as we like, we should remember that God gave the strongest prohibitions about the occult. And the reason for the prohibitions? There *is* power in the occult, as the Egyptian magicians in Moses' time demonstrated, replicating some of the supernatural acts of God. While we might think that dabbling in ouija boards, fortune telling and even horoscopes is harmless fun, God thinks differently, because He knows that there is a dark power that can entrap and confuse us. God spoke in the strongest terms because He wanted to raise up a people who would put their trust in Him, and not in dark forces. And remember that often sexual perversion was part of occultist worship. Admittedly, these words about executing the sorceress have been abused a great deal over the centuries. But that doesn't mean that the sternest warning they contain should be ignored.

To ponder: Why do you think that there is such an interest in the occult today?

God spoke in the strongest terms ...

Those on the margins

BIG PICTURE
Exodus 22:21–27
Isaiah 1:10–17

FOCUS
'Do not take advantage of the widow or the fatherless. If you do and they cry out to me, I will certainly hear their cry.'
(Exod. 22:22–23)

… social justice

sits at the very

heart of the

gospel …

IN RECENT years, the Church has rediscovered the truth that social justice sits at the very heart of the gospel; it is not an addendum, or a part of evangelism ('We'll feed you if you listen to this sermon'). Walking with the poor, protecting their rights and working with them to alleviate poverty are enshrined in the Law, and God is passionate about this. The alien and the widow were the most vulnerable in Israelite culture. An alien – meaning a stranger – had no family property, inherited through the generations, and might be forced to take badly paid jobs in the community. Maybe they would not have had access to the judicial system. And widows and orphans were vulnerable because no man was providing for them.

When it comes to issues of poverty and injustice in our world, we can be tempted to believe that the challenges are too big, and whatever we do, it's just a drop in the proverbial ocean. In his helpful book *Rich Thinking about the World's Poor*, Peter Meadows totally dispels that myth. Over the last 30 years, the developing world has halved the number of infant deaths, and over the last decade, deaths of young children from diarrhoea have also been halved – saving one and a half million lives every year. The number of children getting an education is now outpacing the population growth – more children are going to school than ever before. The world is changing. And God wants His people to play their part in bringing about that change. It's a command, not an option.

Prayer: Lord, show me my part in responding to Your heart for the marginalised. May we echo Your heart of compassion. Amen.

Respect for state leaders

BIG PICTURE
Exodus 22:28–31
Romans 13:1–7

FOCUS
'Do not blaspheme God or curse the ruler of your people.' (Exod. 22:28)

EARLIER I mentioned last year's US presidential election. Almost everybody I spoke to agreed that they were delighted that it was over, whatever their political persuasion. Households are bombarded with automated telephone calls every evening; some people just take the phones off the hook for a couple of weeks. There was broad agreement that the tone of the campaign was vitriolic, as accusations and counter-accusations were volleyed back and forth. And it was not just the candidates who slugged it out, but hundreds of millions of dollars were spent on aggressive television advertising to smear the credibility of both main candidates.

But here's what *really* worried me: Christians waded in too, often circulating emails full of unsubstantiated rumours and comments. I know of Christians who will only pray for their President if he or she happens to represent their party of choice, which frankly shows that their party politics take priority over their kingdom values. In Britain, respect for public service is at an all-time low. God calls His people to respect and honour the leaders He places over them; Romans 13 makes it clear that we should submit to the authority of the state. There are obviously limits to this. When the state demands that we make choices that violate our Christian ethics, then we are right to resist. Respect doesn't mean endorsement or silence; church leaders have often confronted dictators. But when we do challenge, let's do so with a calm, gracious tone, and avoid the temptation to spread slander.

Prayer: Lord, I pray for all those in leadership regardless of their political affiliation. Grant that they might lead well. Amen.

WED 14 AUG

The crowd

FOCUS
'Do not follow the crowd
in doing wrong.'
(Exod. 23:2)

AS GOD calls His people to be exemplary in truth, justice and compassion, there is a twofold warning in these verses that we'd do well to apply – we are often called to break step with the crowd. Christians are called to live as non-conformists, refusing to go along with the popular consensus, because the crowd is often wrong. Crowd power is huge. If a huge number of people believe the same idea, we can be wary of challenging them – how can they all be wrong, and we be right? To break step means that we are made to feel like the odd ones out. But we must think for ourselves. Crowds often suspend their critical faculties, choosing to be lazy about hammering out issues and ethics, and preferring to just settle back and go with the flow.

One example to illustrate my point is the general attitude towards virginity that prevails these days. With movies like *The 40 Year Old Virgin,* Hollywood derides the person who has emerged from their teen years and has chosen not to have sex.

Encouragements towards sexual abstinence are rejected as being oppressive and cruel, as the propaganda machine, that celebrates tolerance, is so intolerant of the few who choose to live their lives to a different standard. If we've any doubt that the crowd is often wrong, witness the way the religious barons of Jesus' day shamelessly manipulated them. The majority is certainly not always right: let's ensure that we don't rush to nod our agreement, and get out of step with the Lord of our lives.

The majority

is certainly not

always right ...

Prayer: Lord, give me wisdom to know when the majority is wrong, and courage to break step with them. Amen.

LIFE is getting busier. We are all scrambling for time to rest with friends and family. Church attendance is now being relegated in our league of priorities. I think that there's real danger here. As we witness God instituting three annual festivals for His people, let's look past the pattern of their gatherings and consider their purpose. Notice that a key word is 'celebrate' – these festivals were lively, creative, fun gatherings, where the corporate memory of God's people was encouraged. They were times of thankfulness, where they reaffirmed that, no matter how hard they had worked, ultimately God was their source. It's easy for us to lose sight of God as the provider of our daily bread. And the festivals were designed to provoke memories, as the people looked back, not in empty nostalgia, but to the God who had saved them, and stood ready to be their protector again.

Life erodes my faith. The incessant beeping of my smartphone, and the jarring headlines of today's newspapers conspire to dilute my hope, and bewilder me. But when I stand shoulder to shoulder with fellow members of the family of God, declare my faith (whatever I feel) in liturgy and song and prayer, and then allow myself to be brought again to the 'straight edge' of God's Word, I am replenished to live out my faith in this noisy techno-jungle.

We're not the first generation to feel the pressure of time. To attend those celebrations was disruptive and costly. But they were vital.

Prayer: Thank You, Father, for creating the Church, the community of Your people. Help me to make its fellowship a priority in my life. Amen.

Celebration time

BIG PICTURE
Exodus 23:14–33
Hebrews 10:19–25

FOCUS
'Three times a year you are to celebrate a festival to me.' (Exod. 23:14)

A creative Creator

BIG PICTURE
Exodus 24:1–11
Exodus 31:1–11

FOCUS

'Moses then took the blood, sprinkled it on the people and said, "This is the blood of the covenant that the LORD has made with you in accordance with all these words."'
(Exod. 24:8)

I'M ALWAYS intrigued by those who resist the work of artists and dramatists in the Church, as if words spoken, especially by preachers, are more significant than theatre. And I've been at the events where drama is used, but it's disconnected from the main activity. I think that this is wrong. Whenever I have the opportunity to serve alongside actors, I want their contribution to be considered to be of equal value: I teach using words, humour and story-telling, and they preach through ingenious scriptwriting and crafted acting.

When I'm challenged about this view, and people ask where God validates creativity in Scripture, I'm tempted to turn to Genesis chapter 1: in the beginning God *created*. In this episode, God used a variety of different methods to firmly imprint the memory of the covenant into Israel's thinking. Words were read, altars were built, there was the smell of sacrifices and then (most unusually of all) blood was sprinkled over the people. All of their senses were engaged in the confirming of the covenant agreement, and then a selected few of them were invited to dine with God.

Similarly, instead of just teaching us that He gave His body and blood for us, new significance was breathed into the Passover meal as Jesus instructed us to walk through the mini-drama of the communion meal. Despite this, so often artists, sculptors and playwrights are frustrated in the word-focused Church, feeling that there is no validation of their gifts or opportunity for them to express them. And that's a tragedy.

Prayer: Thank You for communicating with us in so many ways, Lord. May colour and creativity be celebrated among Your people. Amen.

Waiting for God

Sometimes I wonder if we Christians give the
impression that God is more available than He is.
We're promised that God will never leave nor forsake
us. But does that mean that He is constantly talking
with us? I don't think it's that easy. There are seasons
when it feels God is quiet. I can hear someone rushing
to offer the old cliché, 'If God seem far away – guess
who's moved?' I think it is untrue and has the
potential to hurt people who are already confused
with shame. The implication is if we can't hear God,
then we must have done something wrong – in other
words, we're to blame. But in the midst of all this
wonderful fellowship with God, the meal with the
elders, and the instructions for the building of the
tabernacle, Moses spends six days on the edge of a
cloud, but only on the seventh was he called to enter
into it. Moses spent 40 days communing with God:
but six days of waiting came first. Waiting for God is
part of the Christian life. He's well worth waiting for,
but if you're in that place, may you know grace and
patience while you wait.

**To ponder: What do you think of the adage, 'If God
seems far away, guess who's moved?'**

He's well worth
waiting for ...

God on the move

FOCUS

'The poles are to remain in the rings of this ark; they are not to be removed.' (Exod. 25:15)

THROUGHOUT Christian history, preachers and teachers have looked at the details of the tabernacle and have treated them like an allegory, drawing out all kinds of 'truths' from the tent: a very uncertain way to preach. Allegorical preaching can be speculative because it is left to the preacher to apply and interpret the allegory; our faith should be based on something more substantial than a tabernacle tent peg! That said, there are details in the tabernacle construction that speak of obvious truths. For example, the carrying poles provided for the ark of the covenant were never to be removed. The ark, like the tabernacle itself, which Temper Longman calls 'sacred space for the long haul', was designed to be a portable item. The God who had revealed Himself on the summit of a very static, unmovable mountain, was now committed to moving with His people, to dwell among them, wherever they were.

John, in his Gospel, picks up this word *tabernacle*. When we read that God came and 'dwelt' among us, a better translation is 'God came and tented it among us'. God is a camper. Change shouldn't come as a surprise to us, either in our own individual lives or in the churches of which we are a part. The word *ekklesia*, from which we get the somewhat musty, stuffy-sounding word 'ecclesiastical', means 'the called out ones'. It's an exciting word that describes a people on a mission with the God who is going somewhere. The arrangement still works like this: He leads, we follow.

He leads,

we follow

Prayer: Lord, when change threatens to unsettle me, help me embrace the adventure of following hard after You, wherever You lead. Amen.

The table of
fellowship

BIG PICTURE
Exodus 25:23–40
1 Corinthians
11:23–26

FOCUS
'Put the bread of the
Presence on this table to
be before me at all times.'
(Exod. 25:30)

A MEALTIME can be a delightful experience. Far more than an occasion for the serving and swallowing of food, a meal is intended to be a social event and far more than a human filling station that provides more fuel for the day. The meal table is a place of conversation, laughter, updating, story-telling – and, in our case at the moment with two small grandchildren sharing the table, the opportunity to decorate each other with flying food. Having shared a meal with the elders on Mount Sinai, the abiding imagery that is provided for Israel is that of the meal table, with the bread of the Presence placed upon the table; God in the midst of His people, figuratively speaking, eating and drinking with them. The final event that Jesus had with His disciples, one that was surely burned deeply into their memory, was the shared meal.

All of this points to the kind of relationship that God wants us to enjoy with Him. Here I need to be careful, lest I give the impression that faith is like a happy Sunday lunchtime, with conversation going back and forth. It's not like that, at least for me. God does speak but sometimes not as much as I'd like; for now, I don't see Him across the table clearly. One day there will be another meal, the marriage supper of the lamb, and what a wonderful, face-to-face event that will be. But in the meantime, you and I can come in prayer and mutter our comments, share our updates and stories and requests and tears, and know by faith that we are heard. I'd like to develop that habit of 'lunching' with God more.

Prayer: Lord, help me to walk through today, sharing it with You, and knowing that I'm heard as I do. Amen.

WED 21 AUG

Sacred spaces

BIG PICTURE
Exodus 26:1–37
Psalm 132:13–14

FOCUS
'Set up the tabernacle according to the plan shown you on the mountain.' (Exod. 26:30)

KEEN to reject the notion that church buildings are 'God's houses', where He lives, I have long celebrated the truth that the Church consists of people, not of bricks and mortar. When we succumb to the idea that a special building is 'God's house', then we give the impression that we are going to visit God every weekend. But in recent years I have come to value sacred spaces, places where God has met people, or done something remarkable. God gave His people a 'prophetic tent' in the careful design of the tabernacle. Its fixtures and fittings spoke volumes about God; firstly, that He was majestic and holy. Decorated with cherubim, the Israelites were reminded that they came into the presence of a heavenly court when they came to worship. Then the size of the tabernacle – twice the size of a normal tent – and the colours and textiles used were associated with royalty. The Hebrews needed to remember that they were not without a King, but that their King was actually the King of kings.

The tabernacle acted as a reminder of God's abiding presence, a point of contact with Him, and a tangible token of His promise to be with His people. Surely something similar happens when we gasp in awe at the craftsmanship demonstrated in some of our beautiful ancient church buildings. In a way that I can't explain theologically, there's a sense of God's beautiful presence in those places as our senses are aroused, and we remember that here, God has been worshipped and honoured for centuries. Are there places that are special to you?

Prayer: Lord, thank You for buildings, beaches, hillsides and woodland walks, where I have prayed, made good choices and met with You. Amen.

IT'S an awkward moment that anyone who enjoys offering hospitality has probably experienced. The meal has been shared, the conversation was vibrant and interesting, but now the clock is heading towards the small hours and it's time for the guests to head home – at least you, the host, think so. But they are showing no signs of shifting, and so you stretch, yawn and perhaps ask if their baby-sitters work night shifts. A friend of mine, unwilling to resort to subtlety, used to bring evenings to a swift conclusion with the words. 'Right, it's been great to see you, but let's call it a night, shall we?' With that, we would be swiftly ushered out of the door. The welcome had been warm, but was over!

As we discover that the words 'Tent of Meeting' are used for the first time in this passage, we realise that God is fundamentally social – He wants to meet His people. And the light that was always to be left on indicated His never-ending welcome and presence available. Sometimes when I come to prayer, I wrestle with the idea that God might be bored with me blethering on yet again, and that somehow I have to convince Him to take interest in me and my small concerns. But that is wrong: God is always eager, always interested, and never shows us the door. And the thick curtain of the tabernacle, later found in the Temple, limiting His presence, was torn from top to bottom when Jesus died. The table is set, the light is on, and the curtain has been ripped to allow us all to draw near. Come on in.

Prayer: Lord, by faith, I draw near, knowing that Your welcome to me is not just a duty, but Your delight. Amen.

Always welcome

BIG PICTURE
Exodus 27:1–21
Matthew 27:45–53

FOCUS
'For the entrance to the courtyard, provide a curtain twenty cubits long, of blue, purple and scarlet yarn and finely twisted linen – the work of an embroiderer'
(Exod. 27:16)

FRI 23 AUG

The heart of a leader

BIG PICTURE
Exodus 28:1–43
Philippians 1:1–11

FOCUS

'Whenever Aaron enters the Holy Place, he will bear the names of the sons of Israel over his heart on the breastpiece of decision as a … memorial before the LORD.' (Exod. 28:29–30)

AS WE read about the clothing to be worn by the high priest, notice that the names of Israel were placed close to Aaron's heart. This is a vivid portrait of what true leadership should be like. I've met ministers who say that they love preaching – it's just people they don't like. While everyone has a different temperament, and not everyone functions with the same ease in social situations, surely leadership that doesn't carry the people 'on their hearts' is dysfunctional. There's always a danger that those of us who lead can end up loving the function, challenge and status of leadership. We can forget that, if we don't lead out of genuine love for God's people – and remember that they are not *our* people, but have been entrusted to us – then perhaps we have gone astray. Paul had the Philippians 'in his heart' – that meant he remembered them with affection, prayed for them, and 'longed for them all with the affection of Christ Jesus'. The tough, brave apostle had an incredibly tender heart for the people of God.

But there's a flipside to all of this. Sometimes having others on your heart is a costly business. When those you care deeply for respond with sniping and unjust criticism, then leaders can get cynical and come to expect a rough time from God's people. Trust me – I've met hundreds, maybe thousands, of leaders who have been seriously wounded by the people of God, and they've ended up somewhat bitter and cynical as a result. God give all of us tender hearts for each other, whether we are leaders or followers.

God give all of us tender hearts …

Prayer: Lord, bless Your leaders with a true heart of love for Your people, and protect their hearts as they love and serve. Amen.

Leaders of the opposition   SEP/OCT 2013

They were famous for their piety, sticklers for rules and regulations ... The Pharisees had turned spirituality into a confusing labyrinth. They were also passionate reformers and were looking with expectation for the Messiah to come and rescue them and their nation. At last He did arrive, but instead of welcoming Him with open arms they muttered, conspired and ultimately sought to have Him killed. Jesus very clearly warned us to avoid falling into the trap of Pharisaism lest we end up opposing His work rather than cooperating with it. Join me next month as we consider how we can avoid batting for the opposition.

Obtain your copy from CWR or a Christian bookshop

24/25 AUG

Exodus 29–30 // 1 Corinthians 10:31

Careful

The elaborate preparations for the ordination of the priest, together with the commands about all the various offerings and washings, seem like a million miles from us, especially with all that blood being liberally sprinkled around. And while there are probably lots of insights that could be gained from the various steps that were taken, what really impacts me is the care and detail that was involved. There was nothing slipshod or casual about all of this; the preparations were to be made with meticulous care. We don't always do quite so well when it comes to Church. A church apartment I once stayed in had obviously been furnished by 'donations' of items that were well past their sell-by date and had been incredibly ugly since their creation. It seemed that people had dumped their junk on the church – and got a tax credit for doing so! In everything we do – the materials we print, the sound desks we run, the chairs we provide for people to sit on – let's do the very best we can, and never shrug our shoulders and say, 'It's OK, it's for the church ...'

To ponder: What do you think it means to do 'everything for the glory of God'?

… let's do
the very best
we can …

HOW quickly we forget. The Hebrews had experienced God's amazing intervention, as He protected them from the pursuing Egyptians. They had been treated to a stunning display of His raw power as they gathered at Mount Sinai. But impatience can affect the memory, and now, as Moses was away for a protracted time, communing with God, they decided to take their lives – and their religion – into their own hands. All that we have read about the preparations for the tabernacle and the ordination of priests points to the awesome purity of God. But now, the fickle Hebrews construct a religion for themselves based around a bull: a symbol of brute strength and fertility, but not of holiness. Their new designer religion made no demands. How similar that is to the pick-and-mix approach to spirituality that is so pervasive today. While we should welcome people's openness to spiritual issues, let's not be drawn into the idea that any spirituality will do.

Notice too that the Israelites did not deny that they had received help in escaping Egypt – but they deceived themselves about the source of that help, giving praise to an image they had only just constructed! Sometimes I do exactly the same thing. I ask God to help me, and then, when an answer comes, I subconsciously attribute the answer to a coincidence. I fail to come back to God with grateful thanks, an attitude that troubles Him, as the teaching of Jesus makes clear. Let's have clarity of mind about who we are trusting in – especially when we're in the waiting zone.

Prayer: You are my strength, my source, my provider, Lord. Help me to remember that, especially when I am waiting. Amen.

The golden calf

BIG PICTURE
Exodus 31–32
Luke 17:11–19

FOCUS
'He took what they handed him and made it into an idol cast in the shape of a calf … Then they said, "These are your gods, Israel, who brought you up out of Egypt."' (Exod. 32:4)

TUES 27 AUG

More of You, Lord

BIG PICTURE
Exodus 33–34
Philippians 3:7–14

FOCUS
'Then Moses said, "Now
show me your glory."'
(Exod. 33:18)

IT'S an uncomfortable thought, but I have been facing the fact that the first few years of my Christian life were probably the season of my fastest growth as a Christian. This was a time of great confusion for me. But I had a voracious hunger to learn, and I wonder if we tend to settle down after a decade or two in the faith. We've accumulated a basic understanding about God that will get us by, and we act as if we have come to know most of what we need to know about Him. But that attitude was not true of Moses. Think about the incredible experience he had, spending weeks at a time with God, and blessed with having God address him like a friend. He had witnessed miracle after miracle, and when it comes to revelation and understanding, he was given the very foundations of Judaeo-Christian civilisation. Yet now he asked God to show him His glory!

God responded to that prayer by giving Moses fresh insight into His compassionate and gracious nature (the word used here means pity that one might have for a tiny baby), and He reveals Himself as being slow to anger – a vital character trait for God when you consider the fickle and rebellious nature of His people. Other insights into God's justice, mercy and faithfulness were revealed and reaffirmed to Moses.

However long you and I have been walking with the Lord, we've not begun to grasp the breadth and depth of who He is. It will take eternity to accomplish that. God give us hearts like Moses, who had understood so much, but had a hunger for more of God.

God give us

hearts like

Moses ...

Prayer: Lord, help me never to settle in my knowledge of You. Reveal Yourself afresh to me as I walk with You today. Amen.

THE next few chapters are a virtual repeat of all that has been said before, as the people move now to actually construct the tabernacle. At first glance, it seems quite tedious that God would go through the same set of instructions again, virtually verbatim. But the fact that He did gives us an interesting insight into the human condition, and God's understanding of the way we tick.

Put bluntly, we need to be told the same things repeatedly, because often we don't listen, fail to understand, or forget what we've learned, meaning that we go through life repeating the same old mistakes. Certainly that was the pattern with Israel, as she lurched around from rebellion, repentance, restitution, rebellion, repentance, restitution …

The disciples of Jesus had the same capacity for dullness. Despite the fact that Jesus clearly set out and explained all that was going to happen to Him, they just didn't 'get it'. Their minds had been so schooled in theological ideas about the Messiah that were *not* true, that when Jesus came as the suffering servant rather than the military conqueror, despite all that He carefully explained, it didn't seem to land in their understanding. The finest of explanations don't guarantee obedience or indeed any response.

And the same is true of me. I hate to admit it, but I am still occasionally found learning lessons that I thought had been dealt with years ago. How about you? Does God find Himself in the place of having to say, 'Let's go through this one more time, shall we?'

Prayer: Lord, help me to learn, and then fully grasp truth as I apply what I learn. I don't want You to have to teach me the same lessons repeatedly. Help me, I pray. Amen.

Let me tell you again

BIG PICTURE
Exodus 35–36
2 Timothy 3:1–9

FOCUS
'Moses assembled the whole Israelite community and said to them, "These are the things the LORD has commanded you to do."'
(Exod. 35:1)

THURS 29 AUG

BIG PICTURE
Exodus 37–38
Romans 15:5–6

FOCUS
'Bezalel … made everything the LORD commanded Moses; with him was Oholiab … an engraver and designer, and an embroiderer in blue, purple and scarlet yarn and fine linen.'
(Exod. 38:22–23)

IT FEELS like the credits you see at the end of a movie, where you are told the names of all of those who contributed to the production, from the director to the person in charge of the catering van. All are included in the credits. We heard about Bezalel earlier when we talked about the value of the artists in Church life, but here he is again, and he and his colleague Oholiab are credited for the fine work they had done.

While it's true that we serve for an audience of One, and we don't serve God in order to win human applause, surely it's important to notice that Bezalel and Oholiab's names were recorded for posterity because of their distinct contribution to the tabernacle construction.

At Timberline Church, Colorado, where I am part of the teaching team, there is a strong attitude in our church culture of honouring and thanking those who work hard. Our annual business meetings, which can be a dreaded occasion in some churches, are actually a delight as we take time to thank and celebrate those who have made special sacrifices in time and service for the work of the church. We like to catch people doing something right.

I know what it feels like to be encouraged: just an hour or so ago, I opened a lovely note of thanks from somebody who had read something I'd written. They found it helpful, took the time to be grateful and quite literally made my day. Don't just look at those who work hard and assume that they need no encouragement, that one day they'll get their reward. Find a way to encourage.

Find a way to encourage

Prayer: Lord, may encouragement, gratitude and honour be hallmarks of my life. Amen.

I'M SURE you can spot the phrase that is repeated through this chapter that reviews all the work that had been done. It is 'as the Lord commanded'. The tabernacle was not the product of some creative thinking by the Israelites. The tabernacle was God's idea, and the building of it was followed exactly according to plan – *as God had commanded it*. As we begin to draw our journey through the Exodus to a close, I find myself asking God to deliver me from my own good ideas, and rather firmly plant in me His wishes and commands. Most of the small or major disasters of my life have been spawned by presumption, where I have rushed ahead and assumed that all would be well. And ironically, blessing in the past can make us more presumptive in the present. We develop a false confidence, believing that because what we have touched in the past turned to gold, then gold will always be the result of our foolhardy decisions. That's why I'd like to be more reflective, soak myself in the wisdom that comes from the Word of God, and be sure that, when I know what God is asking, I respond by being obedient. Moses carefully examined the finished product as the quality tester to make absolutely sure that God's directions had been followed to the letter. And he approved.

May my life and yours meet with similar approval. As we respond to the great commission, we invite others, not just to pray a prayer, to receive His love, and to accept His forgiveness – but also to obey everything that He says in their lives too.

Prayer: Lord, today, may I be found obedient. Amen.

By command

BIG PICTURE
**Exodus 39:1–43
Matthew 28:16–20**

FOCUS
'The Israelites had done all the work just as the LORD had commanded Moses. Moses inspected the work and saw that they had done it just as the LORD had commanded.'
(Exod. 39:42–43)

God in the house

At last the work was finished and the tabernacle was completed. The result was far more than a magnificent work of art, a museum built in memory of a God who had once worked on behalf of Israel, but who worked no longer. Instead, we are left with a wonderful picture of the abiding presence of God who now dwelt among His people. He had pitched His tent among them, which, as we saw earlier, is the language of John's Gospel: as Jesus came and pitched *His* tent among us. Just as Matthew ends his Gospel with the promise of God never leaving us, so Exodus concludes with a compelling image of the Lord who was with Israel day and night.

We will never be alone again. There are days when we feel abandoned, when life doesn't make sense, when prayer seems useless and when we wish God would make His presence felt more obviously. There are seasons of the 'long night of the soul' when we hang on tightly to a faith that feels increasingly fragile. But this much is always true, whether our emotions or current experience confirm it or not. God is with us. God is with you. That's not going to change.

To ponder: Why does God repeatedly stress in His Word that He will be with us? What difference does that truth make?

God is
with you